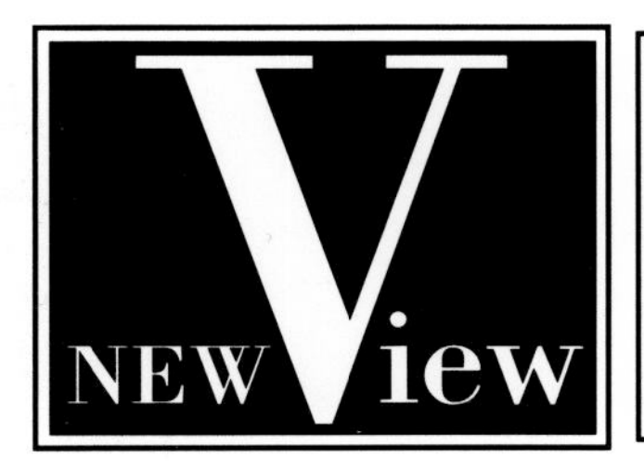

Stars & PLANETS

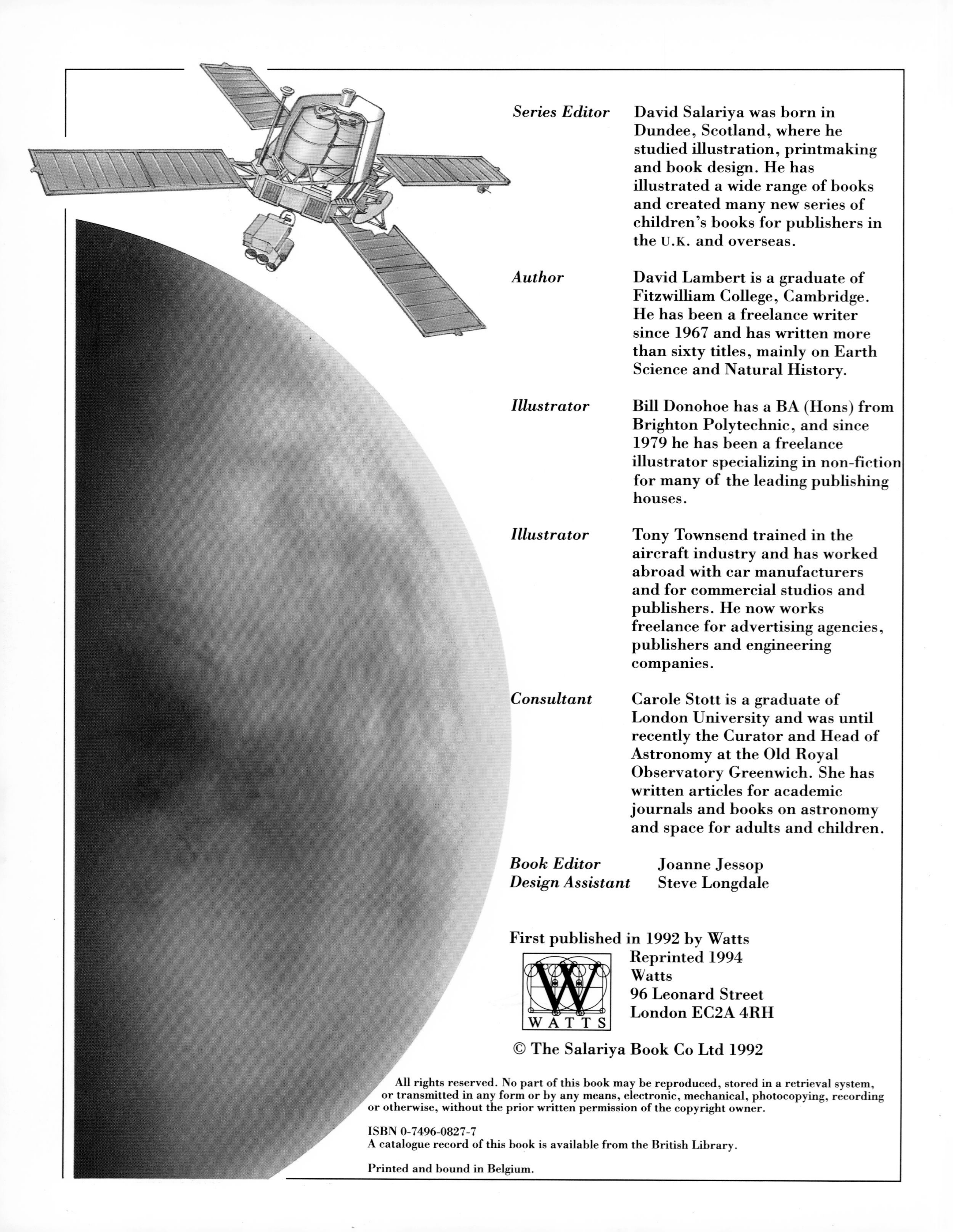

Series Editor David Salariya was born in Dundee, Scotland, where he studied illustration, printmaking and book design. He has illustrated a wide range of books and created many new series of children's books for publishers in the U.K. and overseas.

Author David Lambert is a graduate of Fitzwilliam College, Cambridge. He has been a freelance writer since 1967 and has written more than sixty titles, mainly on Earth Science and Natural History.

Illustrator Bill Donohoe has a BA (Hons) from Brighton Polytechnic, and since 1979 he has been a freelance illustrator specializing in non-fiction for many of the leading publishing houses.

Illustrator Tony Townsend trained in the aircraft industry and has worked abroad with car manufacturers and for commercial studios and publishers. He now works freelance for advertising agencies, publishers and engineering companies.

Consultant Carole Stott is a graduate of London University and was until recently the Curator and Head of Astronomy at the Old Royal Observatory Greenwich. She has written articles for academic journals and books on astronomy and space for adults and children.

Book Editor Joanne Jessop
Design Assistant Steve Longdale

First published in 1992 by Watts
Reprinted 1994
Watts
96 Leonard Street
London EC2A 4RH

ISBN 0-7496-0827-7
A catalogue record of this book is available from the British Library.

Printed and bound in Belgium.

Written by
DAVID LAMBERT

Illustrated by
BILL DONOHOE & TONY TOWNSEND

Created & Designed by
DAVID SALARIYA

London • New York • Sydney • Toronto

CONTENTS

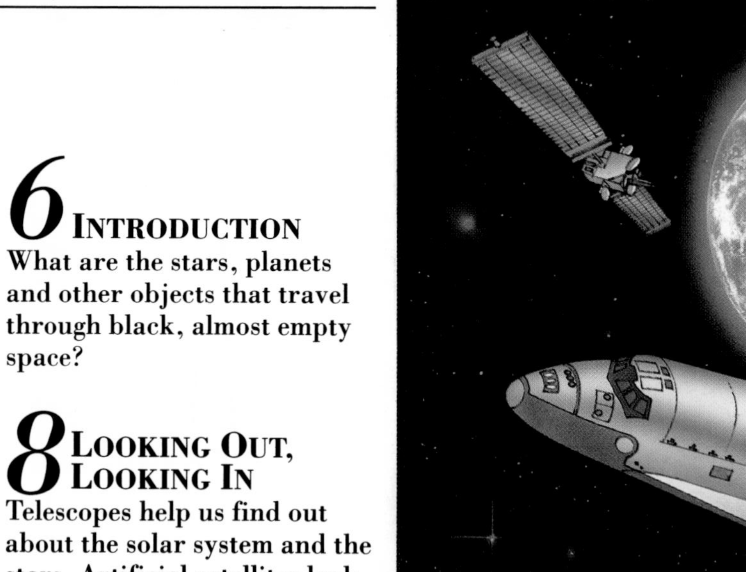

INTRODUCTION

An ant cannot see all the lawn on which it lives. The same used to be true for people living on Earth. We live too near the ground to be able to see the whole planet. In the past, people thought of the Sun as a bright, hot lamp hung in the sky by day. The Moon seemed to be a lamp glowing with a paler, colder light at night. On dark, clear nights stars and planets showed up like billions of tiny twinkling candles. Ancient astronomers believed that all these objects moved around the Earth.

But space travel has given us a new, broader view. Astronauts and artificial satellites orbiting the Earth take pictures showing that we live on a great rocky ball spinning through black, empty space. Powerful telescopes give us more accurate views of worlds beyond our own. We now know that the Sun is a star, a massive fiery ball of gas. Our world and other planets orbit the Sun and shine with its reflected light. Our Moon is a natural satellite that travels around the Earth.

Sun, moons, planets, asteroids (mini planets made of rock) and comets (huge dirty "snowballs") form our solar system. Telescopes show millions of stars beyond the solar system. Great groups of stars called galaxies resemble islands scattered in the blackness. Galaxies, the solar system, the Earth, the Moon, and all other objects including you, form the universe. This book takes you step by step out to the very edge of the universe. In every chapter, illustrations show each outward step.

An outline of the diagram of the universe that appears on the contents page is shown in every chapter; the section that is highlighted indicates which particular part of the universe is now in view.

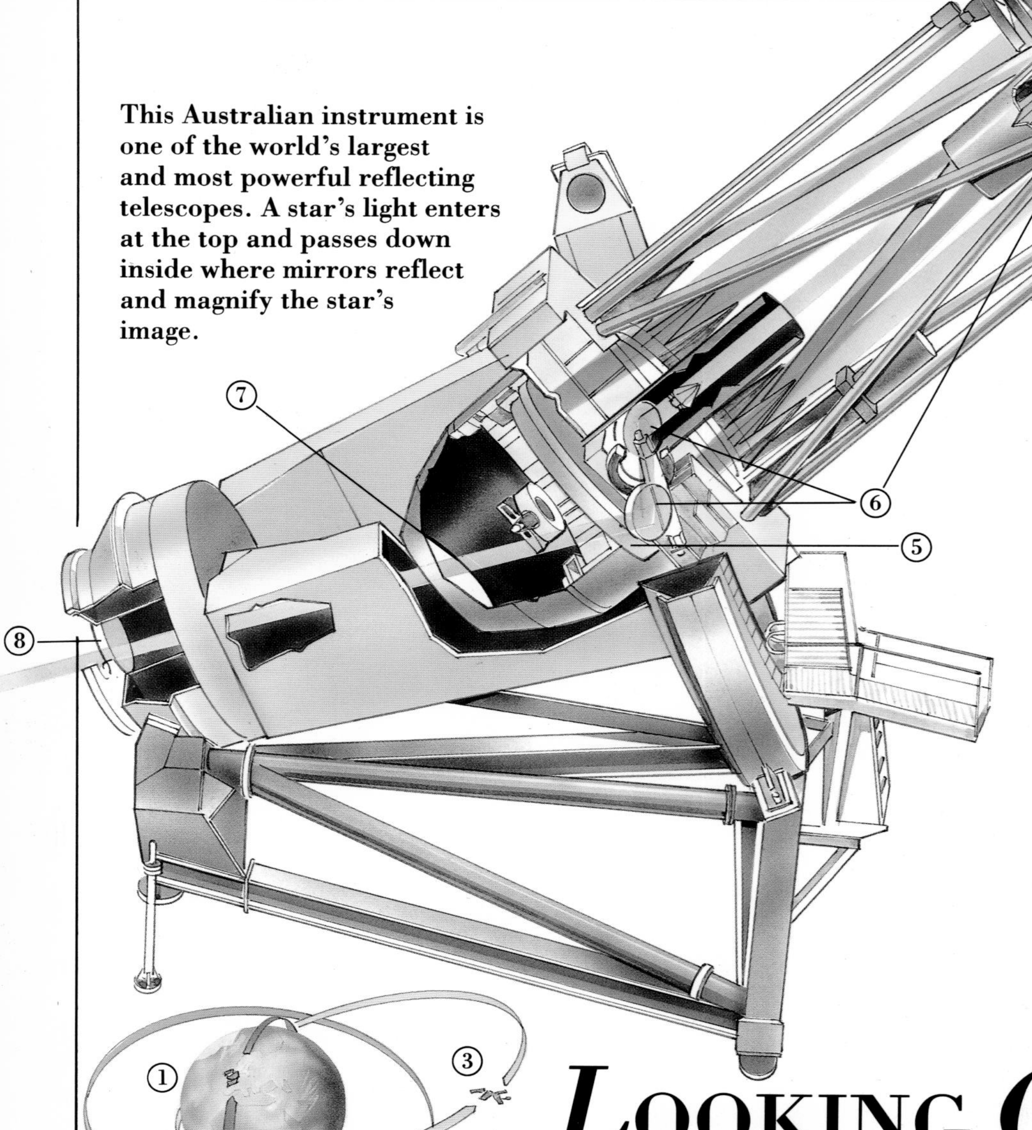

This Australian instrument is one of the world's largest and most powerful reflecting telescopes. A star's light enters at the top and passes down inside where mirrors reflect and magnify the star's image.

Some earth-observation satellites (1) with low orbits around the poles can see all the Earth bit by bit as it spins beneath them. Communications satellites (2) orbit at the same speed as the Earth spins on its axis, so the satellites always stay above the same place on the Earth's surface. Spy satellites (3) have special equipment on board to take close-up pictures of a particular part of the Earth's surface.

Artificial satellites with special instruments can tell us much we did not know about the Earth's air, oceans, lands and cities. The earth-observation satellite shown right can take measurements of clouds, winds and seas. Electricity produced by sunlight shining on its solar panels powers its instruments.

LOOKING OUT, LOOKING IN

Telescopes have shown us much of what we know about the solar system and the stars beyond. Optical telescopes that collect and magnify the light from stars and planets have revealed that these far-off specks are really suns and worlds a bit like ours. Inside a refracting telescope, lenses refract (bend) and magnify light rays that enter one end and can be seen through an eyepiece at the other end. In a reflecting telescope, mirrors reflect light rays that enter one end for viewing through a magnifying eyepiece at the side. Reflecting telescopes can be made bigger and more powerful than refracting telescopes, so they are better at showing and photographing the faintest stars.

Certain telescopes do not use visible light at all. Instead they "see" invisible radiation that stars give off, such as infra-red rays, radio waves and X-rays.

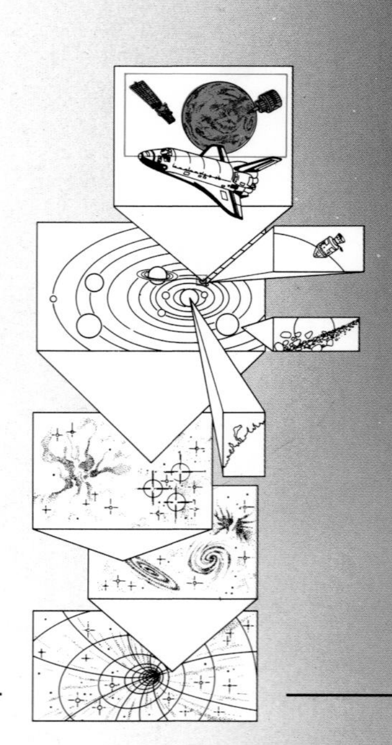

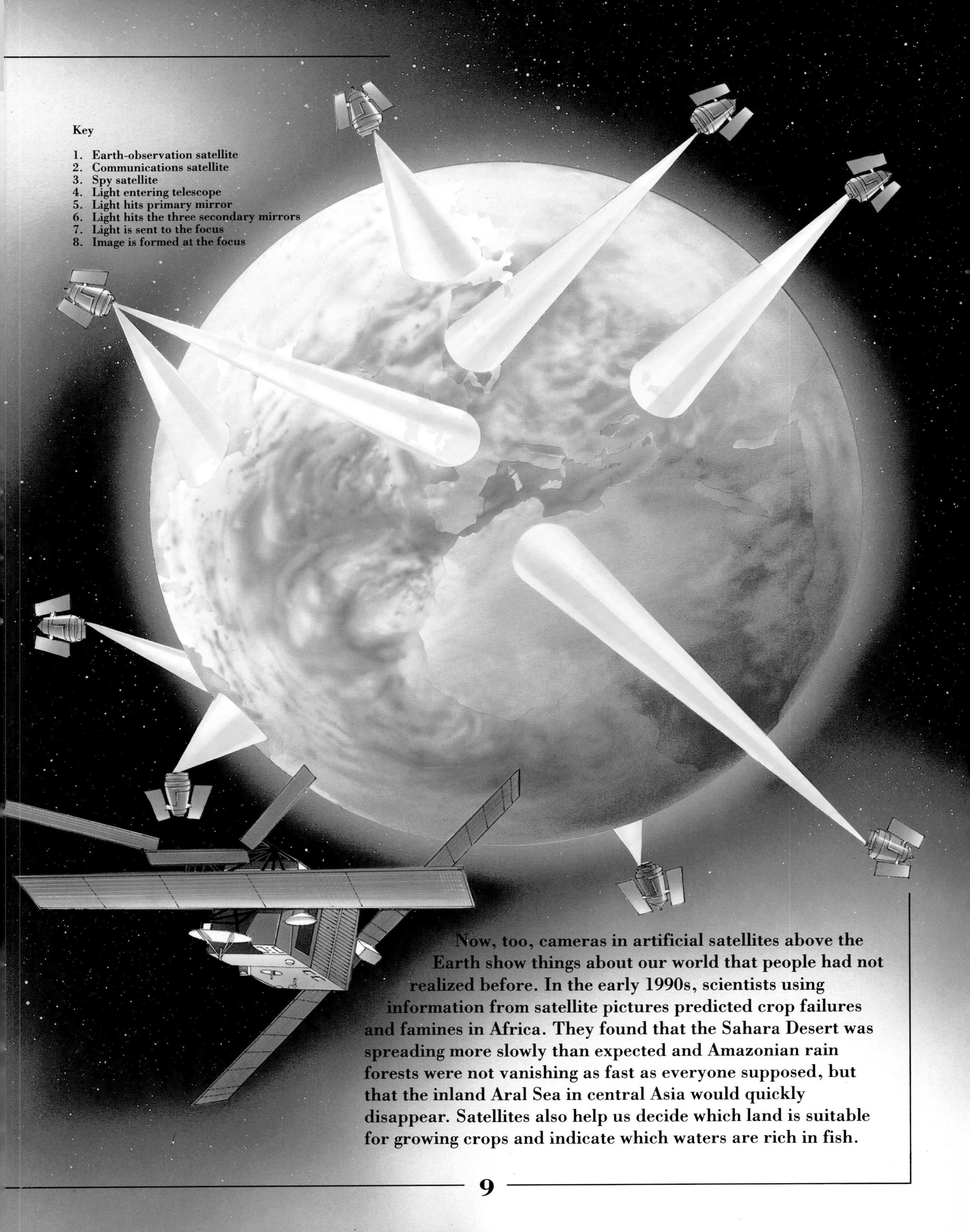

Now, too, cameras in artificial satellites above the Earth show things about our world that people had not realized before. In the early 1990s, scientists using information from satellite pictures predicted crop failures and famines in Africa. They found that the Sahara Desert was spreading more slowly than expected and Amazonian rain forests were not vanishing as fast as everyone supposed, but that the inland Aral Sea in central Asia would quickly disappear. Satellites also help us decide which land is suitable for growing crops and indicate which waters are rich in fish.

WORKING IN SPACE

High above the Earth, trained astronauts can carry out experiments and other tasks that would be impossible down here. First, powerful rockets must thrust these workers in their spacecraft high and fast enough to escape the pull of gravity, which tends to draw all bodies on or near the Earth towards the centre of the Earth. Unlike jet planes, rockets carry their own oxygen for burning fuel, so they can work in airless empty space. But space flight holds dangers for an unprotected human body. Nineteen kilometres high, body fluids start to turn to vapour. Forty-two kilometres high, the Sun's ultra-violet rays are deadly. At take-off, acceleration is so great that a body's weight increases many times. Then, in orbit high above the Earth, acceleration stops, the body weighs nothing and floats about. Spacecraft and space suits enable astronauts to survive all these conditions. Spacecraft also carry enough water, food and oxygen to last their crews for days or even months.

Space shuttles are sent up by rocket thrust and land as giant gliders. The same space shuttle can be used over and over again. Vehicles like this help astronauts launch artificial satellites and space probes, and even capture faulty satellites for repair.

Special rocket backpacks with hand controls let astronauts travel in space outside a space shuttle. They can then catch and bring back faulty satellites.

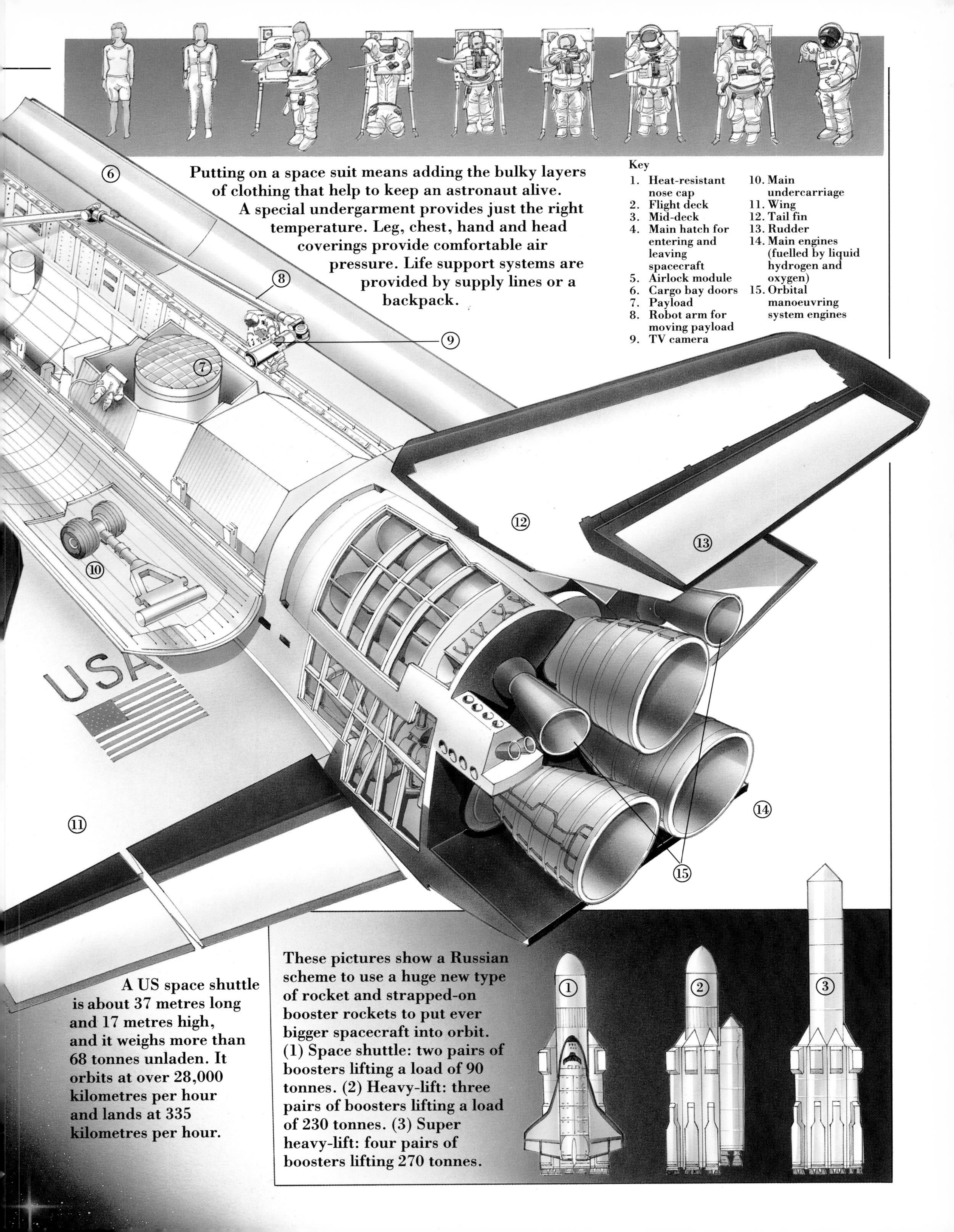

Putting on a space suit means adding the bulky layers of clothing that help to keep an astronaut alive. A special undergarment provides just the right temperature. Leg, chest, hand and head coverings provide comfortable air pressure. Life support systems are provided by supply lines or a backpack.

A US space shuttle is about 37 metres long and 17 metres high, and it weighs more than 68 tonnes unladen. It orbits at over 28,000 kilometres per hour and lands at 335 kilometres per hour.

These pictures show a Russian scheme to use a huge new type of rocket and strapped-on booster rockets to put ever bigger spacecraft into orbit. (1) Space shuttle: two pairs of boosters lifting a load of 90 tonnes. (2) Heavy-lift: three pairs of boosters lifting a load of 230 tonnes. (3) Super heavy-lift: four pairs of boosters lifting 270 tonnes.

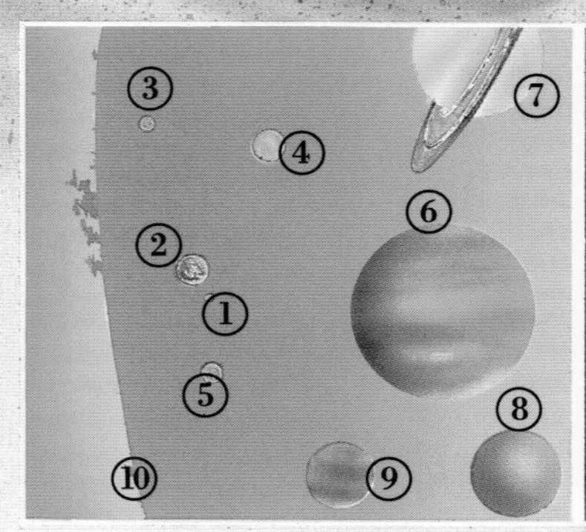

This picture contrasts the size of the Moon (1) with the sizes of planets Earth (2), Mercury (3), Venus (4), Mars (5), Jupiter (6), Saturn (7), Uranus (8), Neptune (9), and their star, the Sun (10).

The Moon might have formed when a Mars-sized mass of rock struck the Earth and broke up. The rock's core fell to Earth, but debris from the mantle was flung into orbit. Gravity brought the debris together near the Earth to form a solid ball: the Moon.

In 1969, the US Apollo programme put the first humans on the Moon with help from the space vehicles shown here. All three vehicles took off from Earth, perched on top of a mighty three-stage system of rockets. As the rockets were used up, they fell away in turn. The modules left behind orbited the Moon. One astronaut stayed orbiting in the command-service module. Two others landed in the lunar module *Eagle*, whose rocket lowered it gently to the Moon's bare rocky surface. Astronauts Neil Armstrong and "Buzz" Aldrin became the first humans to set foot upon a world outside their own. Later the lunar module took them back up to the orbiting command module, which carried all three men safely back to Earth.

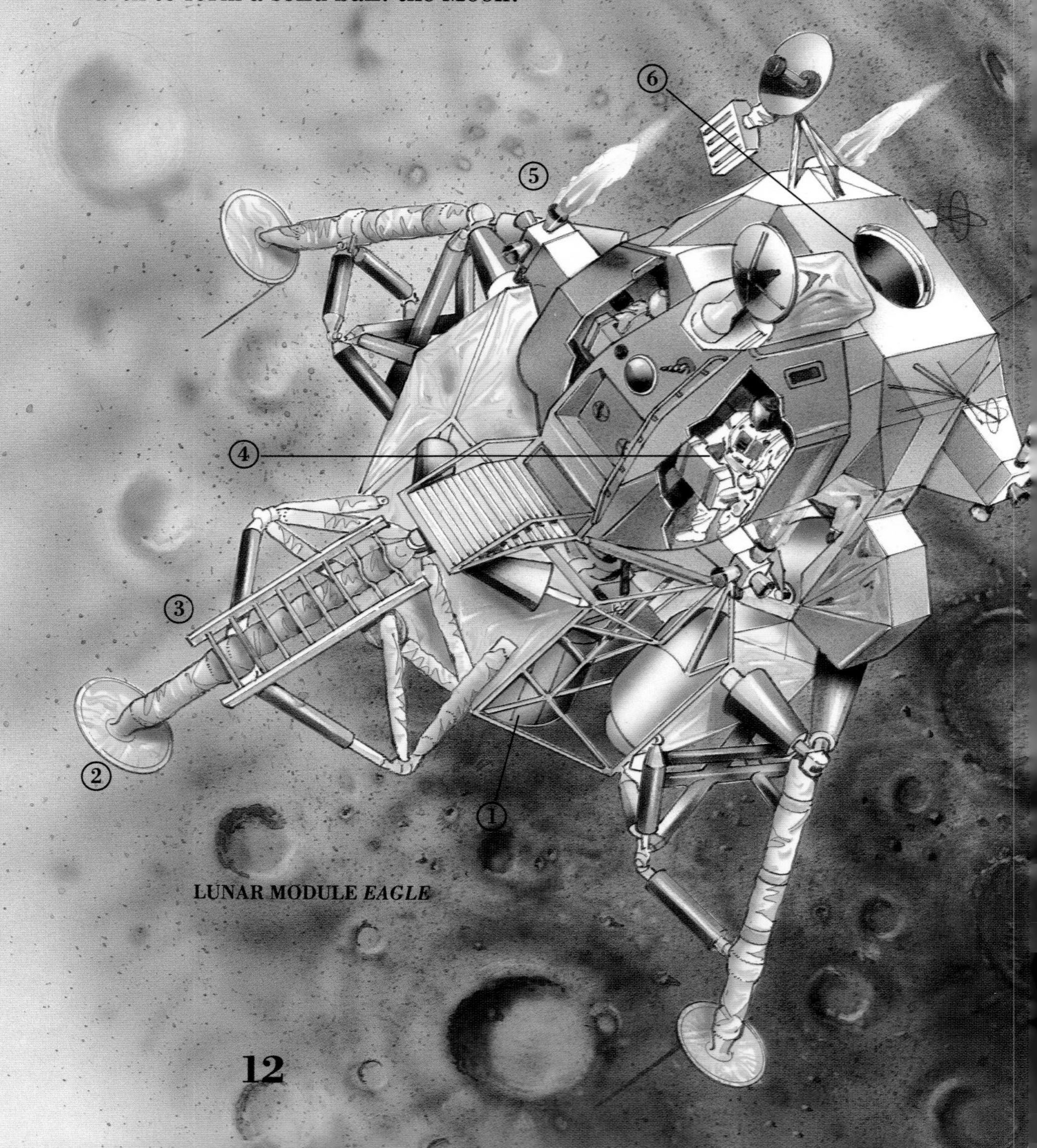

LUNAR MODULE *EAGLE*

THE MOON

Our nearest neighbour in space, the Moon, is only one quarter the Earth's size and travels around it held by the pull of Earth's gravity. Nothing lives on the Moon, a world without air or water. Its dark "seas" are rocky plains of lava that welled up hot and runny from deep down 3500 million years ago and more. Bright areas between the plains are mountains made of rocks as old as any in our solar system. Everywhere the Moon is scarred by craters, large and small. Clavius, among the biggest, is more than 230 kilometres across and 3.6 kilometres deep. Volcanoes created some craters, but most were punched out by lumps of rock and stones that hurtled through space and struck the Moon around 4000 million years ago. Tiny splinters from these accidents formed dust that smothers parts of the Moon.

Scientists believe that the Moon's rocks form three layers: a crust 60 kilometres deep, above a mantle 800 kilometres thick, above an even thicker core.

• A gold olive branch (11), a symbol of peace, was one of several items left on the Moon by *Eagle*'s crew.

EARTH
MERCURY
SUN
VENUS

Average distances from the Sun:
Earth – 150 million kilometres
Venus – 108 million kilometres
Mercury – 58 million kilometres

Key

1. Solar panel
2. Parabolic antenna
3. Magnetometer arm
4. Camera

Spacecraft have peered below the dense Venusian clouds. They sent back images of mountain peaks, craters, volcanoes and lakes and rivers of solid rock formed where molten lava flowed.

EARTH

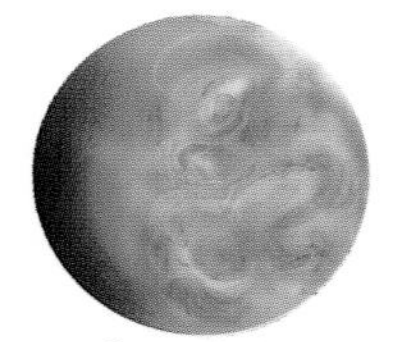

The space shuttle *Mariner 10* passed Mercury twice in 1974 and again in 1975. In March 1974, it sped past on its way out from Earth after first flying by Venus. *Mariner 10* then became a tiny artificial planet orbiting the Sun. As it travelled round the Sun, *Mariner 10* twice more came close enough to Mercury to scan the planet with its television cameras. *Mariner 10* sent back the first clear pictures of Mercury. They showed a Moon-like planet battered by asteroids, most of which fell 4000 million years ago.

• Venus and Mercury are the only planets without moons.

• Venus is the hottest planet. Its average temperature is about 465°C.

• On Venus a day lasts 243 Earth days, but a year lasts 225 days, so a Venusian day lasts longer than a year.

• Mercury has the shortest year of any planet. It takes only 88 Earth days to travel once around the Sun. The planet rotates so slowly that one of its days lasts for most of its year.

• Most planets spin in the same direction as the Earth. Venus spins the other way.

VENUS

①
②
④

MARINER 10

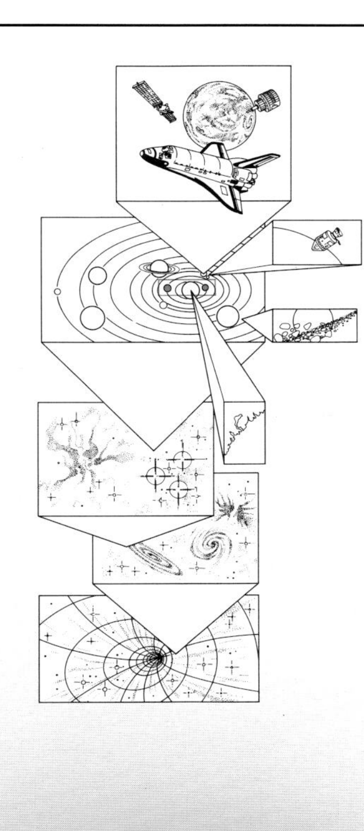

Venus And Mercury

Venus, Mercury, Mars and Earth are called the terrestrial, or "Earth-like", planets. Venus is almost as big as the Earth, but the diameter (measurement through the middle at the widest part) of Mercury is only one-third that of the Earth. No other planets orbit as close to the Sun as Venus and Mercury. Sometimes Mercury is no more than 46 million kilometres away from the Sun.

Clouds loaded with sulphuric acid shed deadly rain that gnaws at the volcanic rocks that cover much of Venus. This planet's suffocating atmosphere of carbon dioxide acts like a greenhouse roof, trapping heat beneath it. Even the coldest parts of Venus stay oven hot. Mercury has hardly any atmosphere to hold in heat, so while its sunlit "day" side bakes, its "night" side cools down enough to freeze a human body solid.

No human explorer plans to visit these deadly worlds, but radar measurements and space probes have told us much about them. We know that meteorite craters pepper Mercury's bare rocky surface and that Venus has giant volcanic mountain peaks and craters, vast lakes of hardened lava and strange criss-cross patterns in its rocks. Like the Earth, both planets are thought to have a solid rocky crust that "floats" on semi-molten rock above a hot, dense metal core.

SUN

MERCURY

The largest scar on Mercury is the Caloris Basin. A ring of mountains surrounds this crater, which is 1300 kilometres across.

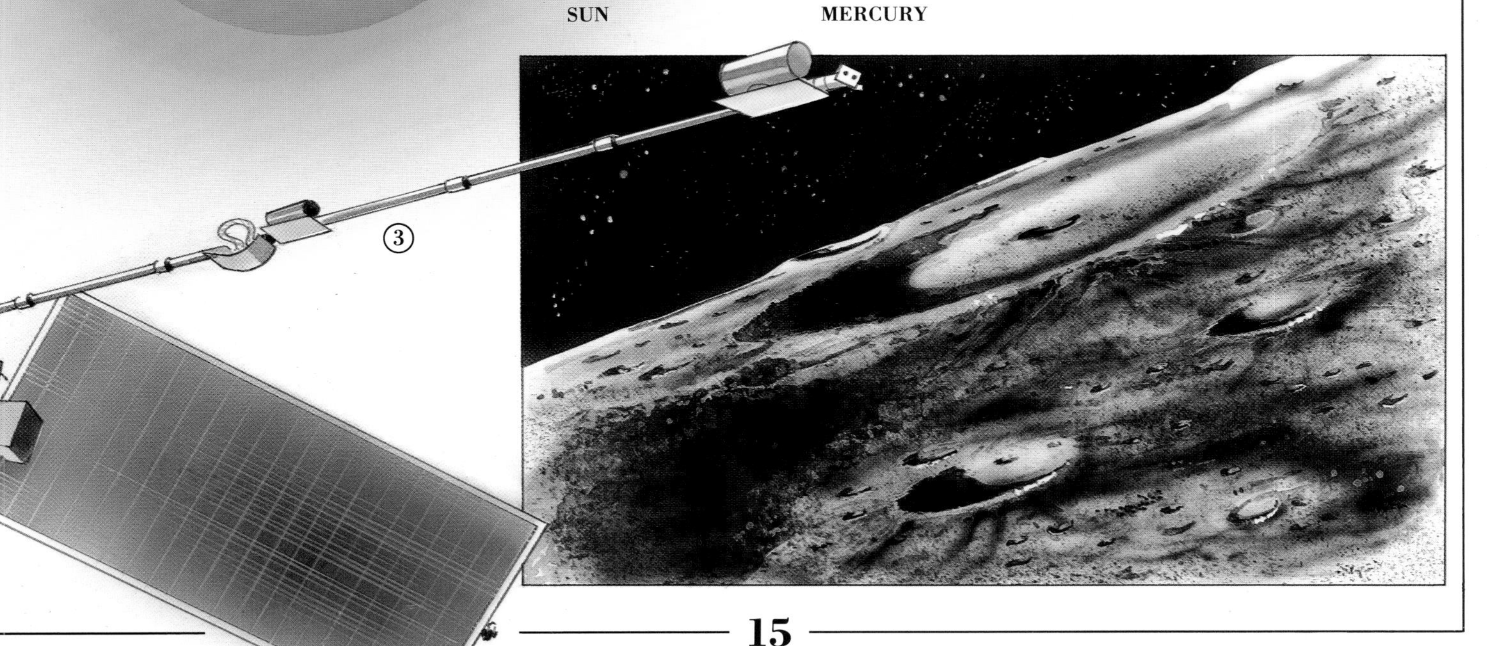

MARS

This reddish planet gets its name from the blood-soaked Roman war god Mars. Mars is the first planet an astronaut would reach after leaving the Earth and zooming away from the Sun. Of all the planets, Mars' surface is the most like the Earth's. Anyone who landed there might be reminded of the red rocks on a stony stretch of the Arizona Desert. Space probes show up rugged mountains, great volcanoes, smooth plains and deep narrow valleys worn out of the rock long ago by running water. Mars even has an atmosphere, with clouds and winds that stir up dust storms, some above its mountain tops.

Mars rotates on its axis about as quickly as the Earth, so day and night on Mars are about the same length as they are on Earth. Mars is even tilted like the Earth, so there are seasons, although these last much longer than ours. In winter, ice caps spread out from the poles.

A closer look shows that Mars is very different from our world. Its diameter is little more than half the Earth's, and Mars is estimated to be one-ninth as heavy as the Earth. So low is its force of gravity that on Mars an adult astronaut would weigh no more than a child weighs here. The Martian atmosphere, mainly carbon dioxide gas, is thin and unbreathable. Martian ice caps are formed largely from frozen carbon dioxide; all liquid water evaporated long ago. Much of Mars is always very cold. Before the Sun rises, even the Martian equator is chillier than the coldest place ever known on Earth.

• Rusty iron-rich stones and dusty soil give Mars its reddish tinge. It has some of the largest volcanoes in the solar system. One is 26 kilometres high. The great cracks in its surface include one that is 4000 kilometres long. This is ten times longer and four times deeper than the Grand Canyon of North America.

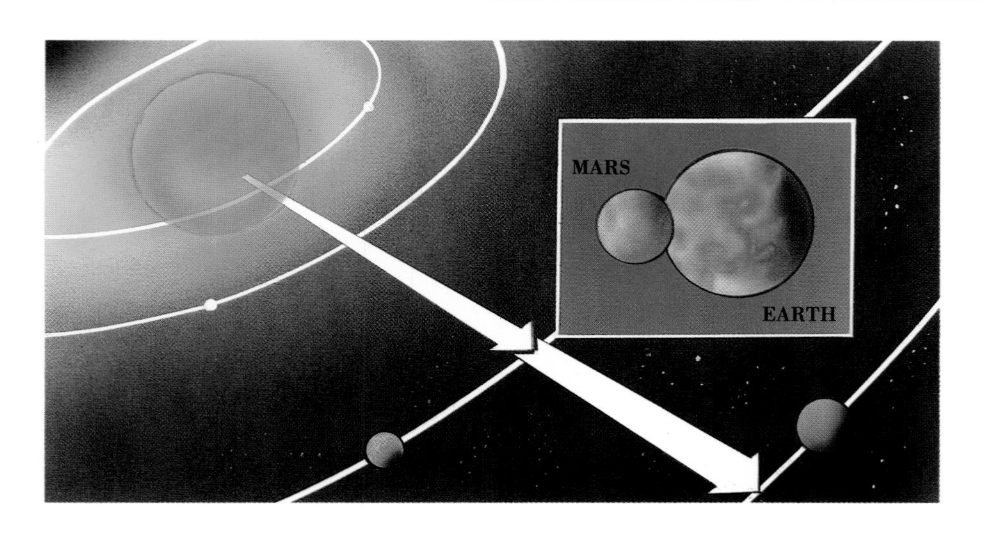

Of the four terrestrial planets – Mercury, Venus, Earth and Mars – Mars is farthest from the Sun: about 228 million kilometres away (twice as far as Venus). The inset picture compares Mars and Earth for size and shows that Mars is far smaller.

Scientists think Mars was once far warmer and wetter than it is today. Its climate changed when meteorites crashed into it and stripped away most of its atmosphere. Not enough remained to trap much of the Sun's heat or to stop water from boiling away into space. Despite these harsh conditions, scientists expect that one day people will set up thriving colonies on Mars.

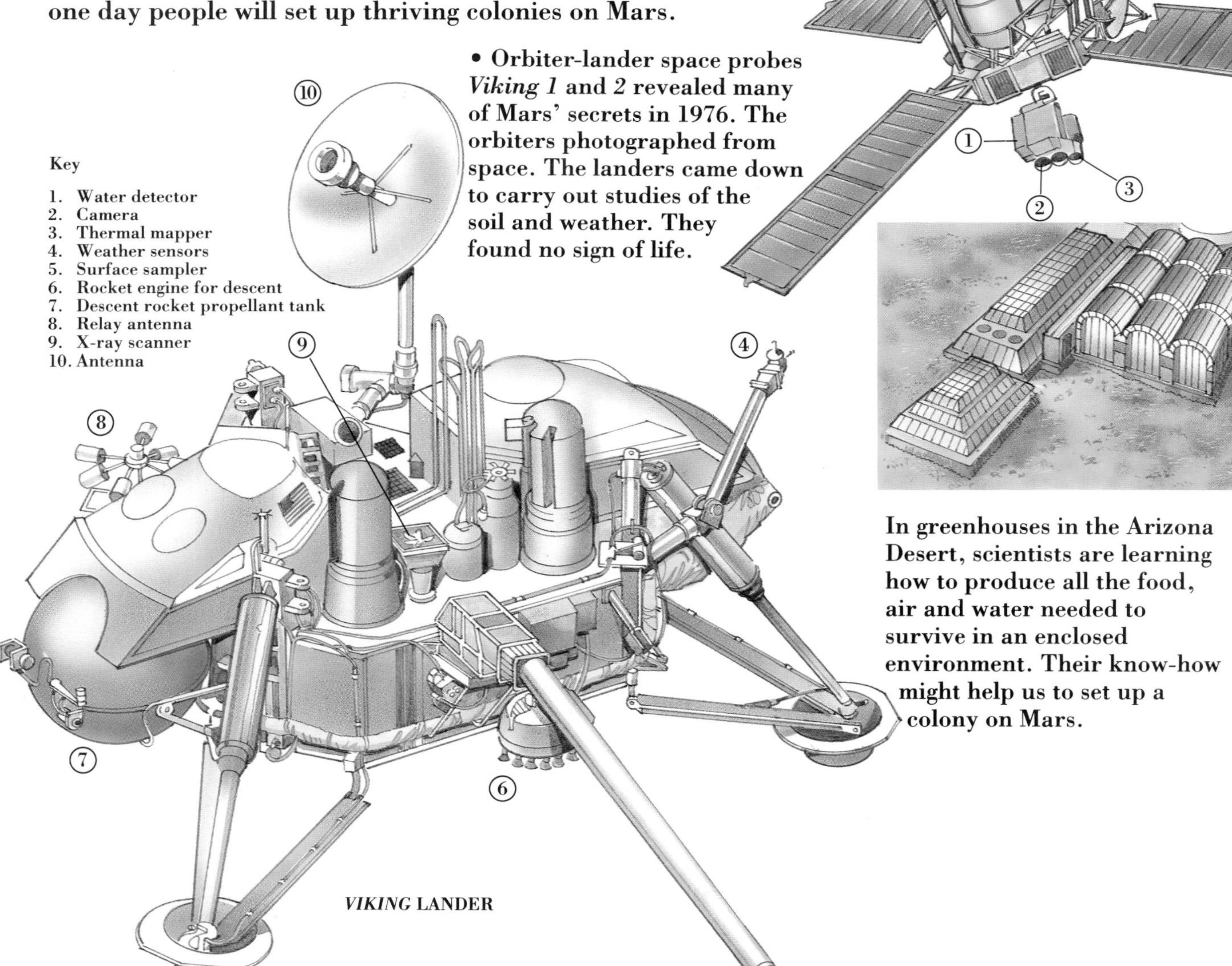

Key

1. Water detector
2. Camera
3. Thermal mapper
4. Weather sensors
5. Surface sampler
6. Rocket engine for descent
7. Descent rocket propellant tank
8. Relay antenna
9. X-ray scanner
10. Antenna

• Orbiter-lander space probes *Viking 1* and *2* revealed many of Mars' secrets in 1976. The orbiters photographed from space. The landers came down to carry out studies of the soil and weather. They found no sign of life.

In greenhouses in the Arizona Desert, scientists are learning how to produce all the food, air and water needed to survive in an enclosed environment. Their know-how might help us to set up a colony on Mars.

Tektites are small glassy objects weighing up to 10 grams that formed when big meteorites punched craters in the Earth's crust. The force of impact melted surface rocks and splashed tiny blobs of molten rock high into the air. Some blobs zoomed up into freezing space. There they cooled and hardened into tiny balls. As these fell back again, air friction remelted them into button and teardrop shapes.

This illustration shows how the asteroid belt looked when the solar system was formed about 4500 million years ago. The density of the asteroid belt was about 2000 times greater than it is today.

ASTEROIDS AND COMETS

Outside the orbit of the planet Mars a ring of rubble travels around the Sun. The largest lump is a rock called Ceres, which is 920 kilometres in diameter. The smallest bits are simply particles of dust. Scientists now know that thousands of asteroids, or minor planets, trace paths through space. Most follow tracks between the planets Mars and Jupiter. A few take long, looping paths that sometimes bring them close to Earth. From time to time lumps of space rock collide with the Earth. Huge craters in Australia, Canada and the United States show where they struck long ago. Each day billions of specks no bigger than a sand grain burn up on entering Earth's atmosphere. Many of these meteors briefly glow as "shooting stars". Lumps of space rock that actually land are meteorites.

Some shooting stars are the broken scraps of giant space "snowballs", known as comets, which orbit the Sun. Each comet's nucleus, or core, is a solid lump of ice and frozen gases mixed with dust and rocks. As a comet nears the Sun, the heat drives off dust and gas as a glowing tail pointing away from the Sun.

THE OUTER PLANETS

Beyond the asteroid belt, lie five remote and strange planets, each named after an ancient Greek or Roman god. First comes Jupiter, then Saturn, Uranus, Neptune and Pluto.

The first four of these outer planets are lightweight giants made up largely of gas, without a solid surface. Jupiter is the solar system's biggest planet, twice as large as all the rest combined. Even Saturn is the size of 95 worlds like ours. At least sixteen moons whizz around Jupiter, and more than twenty orbit Saturn, along with billions of bits of ice aligned in rings like the grooves on a long-playing record. Rings and moons also orbit the third and fourth largest planets, Uranus and Neptune.

The planet remotest from the Sun is Pluto, nearly forty times farther out than the Earth. Pluto is the coldest, tiniest planet, smaller than our Moon and made up largely of ice. A large moon, Charon, orbits Pluto. Scientists think Charon and Pluto were moons that once orbited the planet Neptune and then escaped.

JUPITER

Our main picture shows the outer planets – Jupiter, Saturn, Uranus, Neptune and Pluto – in order, going outward from the Sun.

Their diameters are as follows:
Jupiter – 142,900 kilometres
Saturn – 120,500 kilometres
Uranus – 51,100 kilometres
Neptune – 49,500 kilometres
Pluto – 2300 kilometres

• Jupiter's diameter is 11 times that of the Earth. But it would take 318 Earths to make up Jupiter's weight because it consists largely of lightweight hydrogen. Saturn is light enough to float on water.

PLUTO

NEPTUNE

URANUS

SATURN

GANYMEDE

IO

Two of Jupiter's moons, Ganymede and Io, are among the largest in the solar system. Ganymede is even bigger than the planet Mercury, and Io is roughly the same size as the Earth's Moon. Ganymede seems covered by dark rocks separated by pale bands of frozen slush. Io's colour comes from sulphur. Jets of hot sulphurous vapours spurt more than 300 kilometres above its surface.

• Jupiter's year lasts 11.9 Earth years; Saturn's year lasts 29.5; Uranus's year lasts 84; Neptune's year lasts 165; and Pluto's year lasts 248.5.

• Uranus spins on its side, not in the almost straight-up-and-down position of the rest of the planets. As a result, one part of Uranus has sunlight on it for 42 years; the other is in darkness for 42 years.

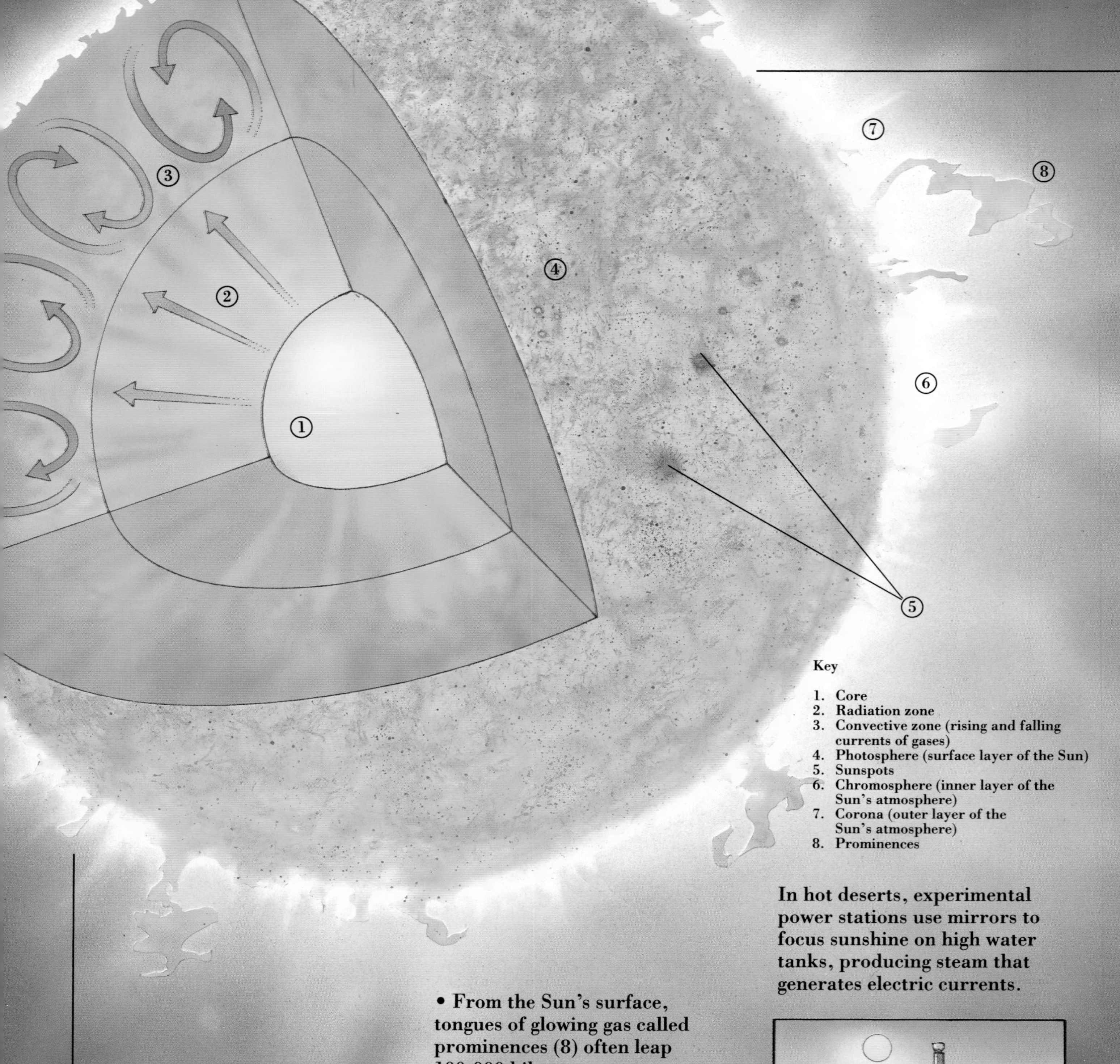

In hot deserts, experimental power stations use mirrors to focus sunshine on high water tanks, producing steam that generates electric currents.

- **From the Sun's surface, tongues of glowing gas called prominences (8) often leap 100,000 kilometres out through space.**

- **Sunspots (5) are relatively cool, dark patches on the surface of the Sun. Many measure about as far across as the Earth.**

- **From the Sun a solar wind of energetic particles blows out far beyond the Earth. The Sun gives off radio waves, ultra-violet waves and X-rays.**

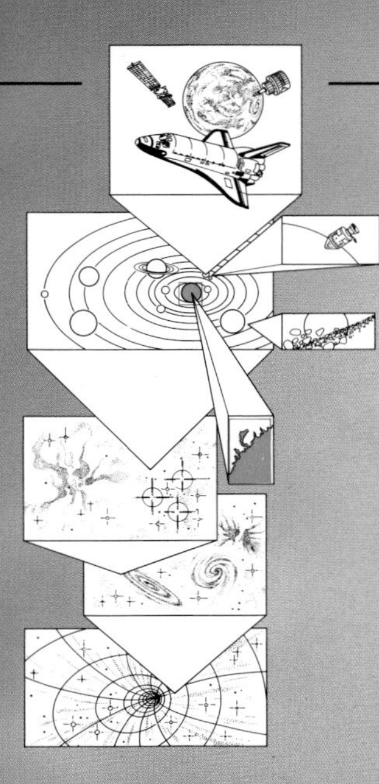

THE SUN

In the middle of the solar system lies by far its largest, heaviest, hottest and brightest object. A million Earths could fit inside this fiery ball of gas – the star we call the Sun. If you could weigh the solar system, the Sun would be more than 700 times heavier than all its moons and planets put together. So great is its mass (the amount of matter it contains) that its pull of gravity is very great indeed. The Sun attracts the planets speeding by so strongly that they go on travelling around this star instead of shooting off through space.

Hot objects give off light as well as heat, and the hotter an object the brighter it glows. The surface of the Sun is a sizzling 5500°C. Its core is hotter still at 14,000,000°C. Even on Earth, 150 million kilometres away, the Sun's heat can burn people's skins and its light is bright enough to blind forever anyone who looks directly at the Sun. The Sun's heat and light come from nuclear reactions in its core. Here, hydrogen nuclei fuse together forming helium and releasing vast amounts of energy. On Earth the same things happen when a hydrogen bomb explodes. The Sun has been "exploding" for around 5000 million years and will go on for 5000 million more before it uses up all its fuel and dies.

In the future, space gadgets may be able to give us extra energy from sunshine. The illustration below shows a mirror lighting cities, solar-power satellites beaming energy to Earth and to factories in space and an energy mirror bouncing power from place to place.

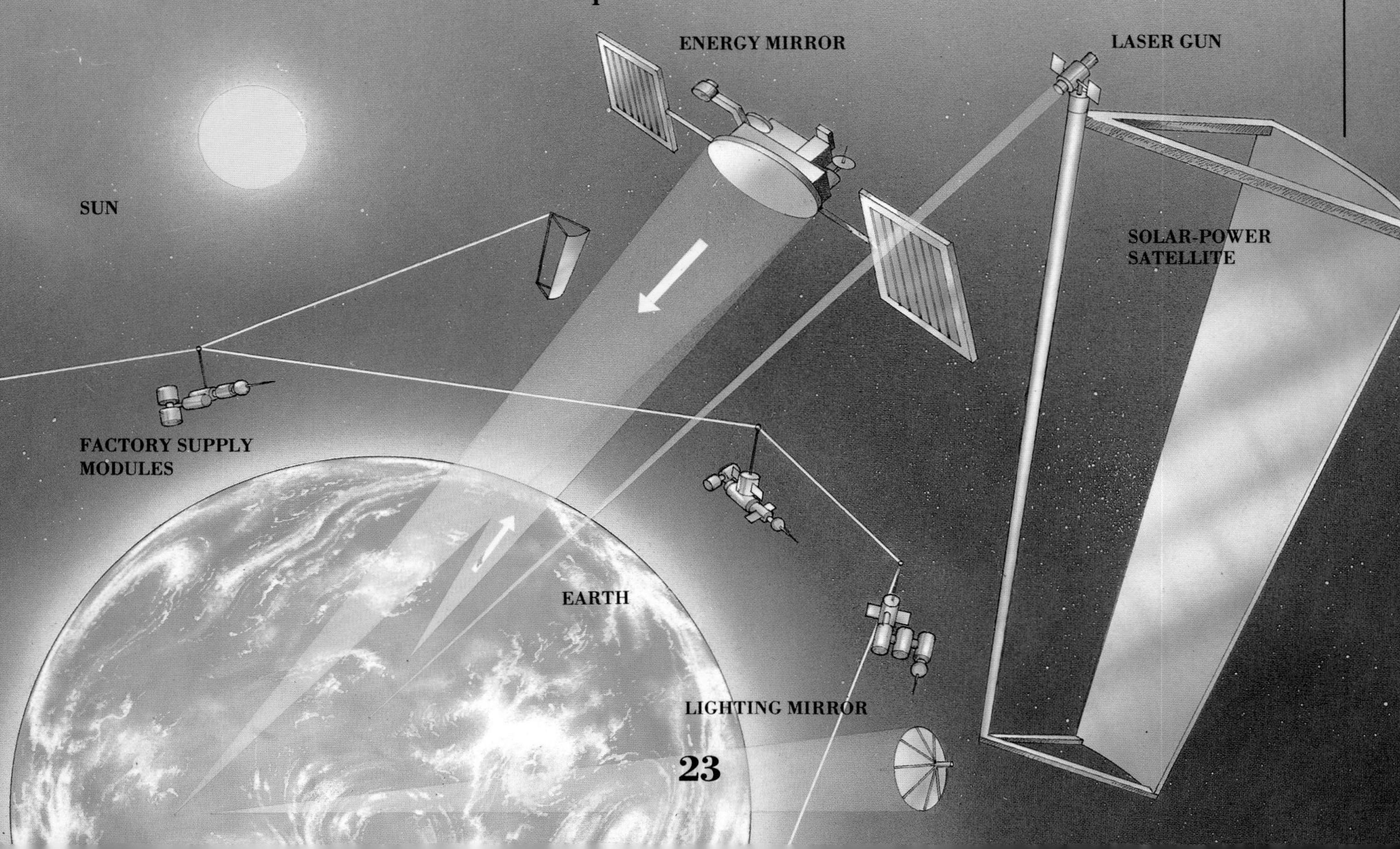

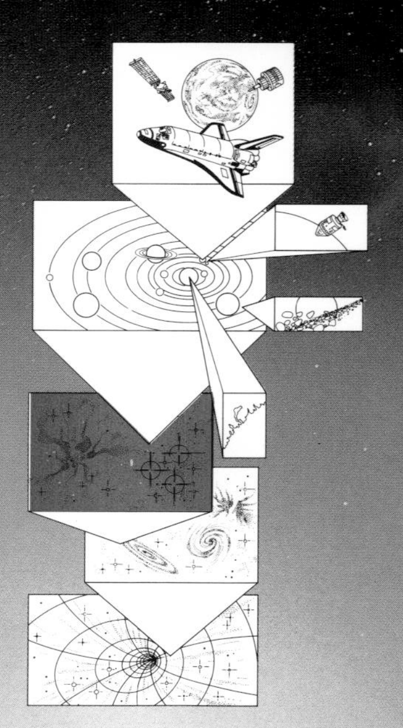

NEBULA

Young stars can be seen in groups known as open clusters. Astronomers have found hundreds of open clusters. Some hold more bright stars than others.

OPEN CLUSTER

STARS BEYOND OURS

On clear nights you can see the tiny winking lights of several thousand stars. A telescope would show you many more. Billions of these mighty balls of glowing gas shine deep in space. They look small only because they are so far away; some giant stars are so big they would stretch out as far as Jupiter's orbit. The nearest star beyond the Sun is more than four light-years from the Earth. (A light-year is about 9.5 billion kilometres – the distance that light travels in one year.) The light now reaching Earth from the remotest stars set out more than 10,000 million light-years ago.

Many of the stars we see might not be there any more. No star lasts forever. Like people, stars are born, mature, grow old and die. They begin to form in clouds of gas and dust called nebulae. Here, gravity pulls billions of particles together in huge balls. The inward pressure heats up these ingredients until nuclear reactions start and a star is born. The hydrogen gas in a star is used up first and turns into helium. As its fuel is used up, a star moves from middle age to old age. Some stars swell into red giants or supergiants, later fading and shrinking into cool white dwarfs as small as the Earth. A massive star can collapse in a huge explosion called a supernova.

PULSAR

Pulsars are the remains of giant stars that exploded. They are tiny stars no bigger than a city and most produce short bursts (pulses) of radio waves. Pulsars are made of tightly packed subatomic particles called neutrons; one cupful would weigh billions of tonnes.

Sometimes a bright "new" star shines briefly in the sky. This supernova is really a giant star burning out in an immense explosion. The material from the supernova is scattered through space. Such stardust helped to build our planet and our bodies.

RED GIANT

WHITE DWARF

BLACK DWARF

One day our aging Sun will swell into a red giant swallowing Mercury and killing all life on Earth. Then the Sun will shrink into a dim white dwarf no bigger than the Earth. Later still it will cool down to a black dwarf – a cold, dark, dense burned-out ember.

SUPERNOVA

STAR ISLANDS IN SPACE

Gazing up at night you see a milky-looking band of starlight in the sky. This is the Milky Way, at least 100,000 million stars that form one great star system, called a galaxy. Our Sun and its planets are just a tiny part of the Milky Way. The pulling force of gravity exerted by its stars holds it all together. Our Galaxy seems to be a narrow band only because we see its stars edge on. If you could look down upon the Galaxy you would see that it is pancake-shaped. In fact, it resembles a gigantic pinwheel (Catherine wheel) 100,000 light-years across. The pinwheel's curving arms consist of stars that together circle the centre of the Galaxy. Our own Sun speeds along at 250 kilometres a second. Even at that speed the Sun takes more than 220 million years to travel once around the middle of the Milky Way.

Beyond the Milky Way lie other galaxies. Some are spiral galaxies like ours. Some are elliptical galaxies, shaped like a football or a rugger ball. Other galaxies have irregular forms. About thirty galaxies, including the Milky Way, make up a cluster in space. Our own cluster, called the Local Group, is 5 million light-years across. More clusters of galaxies lie beyond ours. Astronomers believe that space holds as many as 9000 million galaxies: star islands scattered through a sea of virtual emptiness.

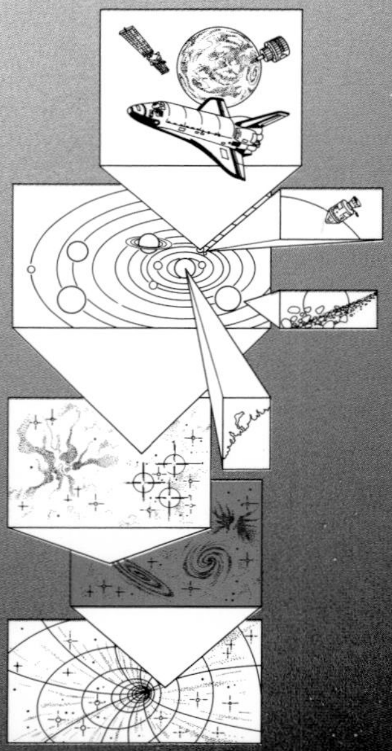

MILKY WAY (a spiral galaxy)

The Milky Way might look like this if you could look at it from space. In one of its vast spiral arms is the Sun surrounded by its planets.

In a spiral galaxy, stars form arms that curve out from the centre. Spiral galaxies have old and young stars, gas and dust.

An elliptical galaxy is a collection of stars in the shape of a football or a rugger ball.

SPIRAL GALAXY

ELLIPTICAL GALAXY

IRREGULAR GALAXY

Irregular galaxies seem to have no special shape. Some of them show up as strange blobs with threads flung out into space as if by vast explosions. Irregular galaxies hold great quantities of gas and dust. The Magellanic Clouds are two famous small irregular galaxies that travel with the Milky Way through space.

Some astronomers believe a black hole lies in the middle of our Galaxy. A black hole is thought to be the very dense remains of a massive star that has collapsed to pinpoint size. So strong is its pull of gravity that light and matter entering a black hole are unable to escape.

In the 1960s American scientists built this giant horn-shaped radio antenna to receive signals from artificial satellites. The researchers were annoyed when the antenna picked up a mysterious radio hiss. Only later did they learn that this hiss was made by the universe when it was very hot and young. It is the Big Bang's dying "sound".

The Cosmic Background Explorer (COBE) satellite investigates background radiation created when the universe was born. In 1992, COBE showed parts of the universe becoming lumpy enough to form galaxies. This and other evidence support the Big Bang theory.

THE EDGE OF THE UNIVERSE

People have often wondered how the stars and planets and all the other objects making up the universe began. Some scientists once argued that the universe as we know it had always been there. Others came to think that its ingredients had once been crammed into a space no bigger than a pinpoint, then a giant explosion scattered everything through space.

Most astronomers now think that 15,000 million years ago the Big Bang created space, time, energy and matter. Some experts have worked out that after a tiny fraction of a second the universe had grown no larger than a pea. After one-hundredth of a second the pea-sized universe had mushroomed to the size of our Sun. Its tiny particles had not clumped together to form anything as big as atoms, although less than two minutes after the Big Bang certain particles were forming the nuclei (cores) of hydrogen and helium atoms. But it probably took 300,000 years for these lightest kinds of atoms to evolve. From them, in time, came all the rest. Billions of hydrogen atoms began building the first stars and galaxies perhaps 12,000 million years ago.

What will happen in the future? The universe might just go on expanding. Or, after billions of years, it might shrink back into a pinpoint before another big bang starts it off again.

GLOSSARY

Asteroid
A rock that orbits the Sun but is smaller than a planet.

Atmosphere
The gases surrounding a star, a planet or a moon.

Axis
An imaginary line through the centre of a planet. Each planet spins on an axis that is tilted at an angle to its orbit.

Black dwarf
The small black ember of a completely burned-out star.

Black hole
A giant star collapsed into a dense, dark tiny object with a force of gravity so great that not even light can escape.

Chromosphere
The part of the Sun's atmosphere just above its photosphere.

Comet
A mass of dust and frozen gases speeding around the Sun.

Corona
The thin gas that forms the Sun's outer atmosphere.

Day
In astronomy, the time a planet takes to make one complete rotation on its axis.

Equator
An imaginary line around the middle of a moon or planet, half way between its poles.

Gravity
A force of attraction that tends to pull two objects together. Your weight is the force exerted on your body by the Earth's gravity.

Light-year
The distance that light travels in one year (9,460,528,405,000 kilometres).

Mass
The amount of matter an object contains. Mass is different from weight. Astronauts lose weight in space but their mass stays the same as on Earth.

Meteor
A particle that falls from space and glows as it burns up in the Earth's atmosphere.

Meteorite
A rocky lump arriving from space onto the surface of a planet or moon.

Milky Way
The galaxy that includes our own solar system.

Moon
A large mass of rock or ice orbiting a planet.

Nebula
A cloud of gas and dust.

Nuclear reaction
What happens when the cores, or nuclei, of atoms join or split. Nuclear reactions release vast amounts of energy.

Open cluster
A group of young stars.

Orbit
One object's path around another, for instance, the Earth's path around the Sun.

Photosphere
The Sun's fiery surface.

Planet
A large object orbiting a star, for instance, the Earth, which orbits the Sun.

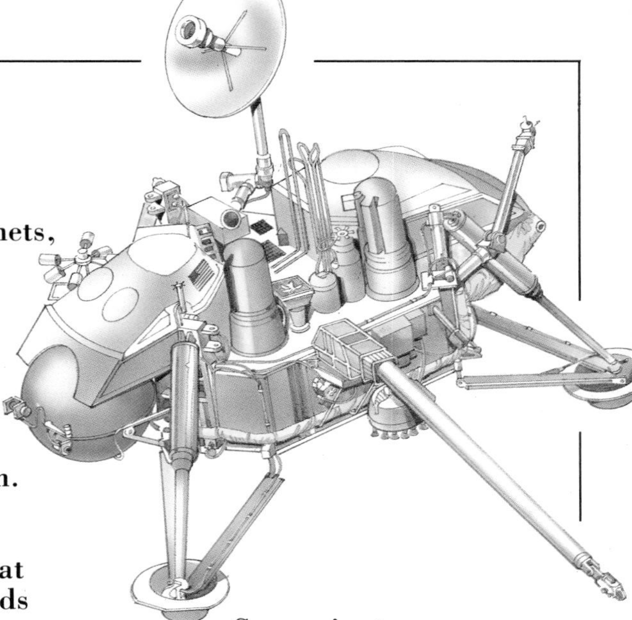

Poles
The imaginary ends of the axis through the middle of the Earth, or any other planet or a moon.

Prominence
A great tongue of glowing gas that rises from the Sun.

Pulsar
A very small, dense star producing brief pulses of radio waves.

Radiation
Different forms of energy rays that include radio waves, infra-red waves, visible light, ultra-violet waves and X-rays.

Red giant
An aging star that swells up and turns from yellow to red as it begins to cool.

Rocket
An engine that moves forward by thrusting burning gases backwards. Rocket engines work even in the emptiness of space.

Satellite
A natural or artificial body orbiting a planet.

Shooting star
Another name for a meteor.

Solar system
The Sun's family of planets, moons, asteroids and comets that orbit it.

Solar wind
A stream of electrically charged particles from the Sun, speeding out through the solar system.

Space probe
An unmanned device that travels in space and sends back to Earth information about other parts of the solar system.

Space shuttle
A reusable type of manned spacecraft first developed in the United States.

Star
A huge, intensely hot, bright ball of gas such as the Sun. Some stars are even bigger and hotter, though very old stars tend to cool and shrink.

Sunspot
A relatively cool, dark patch on the Sun's surface. Sunspots can last for hours or months.

Supergiant
A massive star that swells up far larger than a red giant as it ages, cools and glows less brightly.

Supernova
A massive star collapsing in a giant explosion. Seen from Earth, a supernova seems to be a bright new star.

White dwarf
A red giant or supergiant star that has cooled, faded and shrunk until it is no bigger than the Earth.

Year
The time taken by a planet to travel once around the Sun.

INDEX

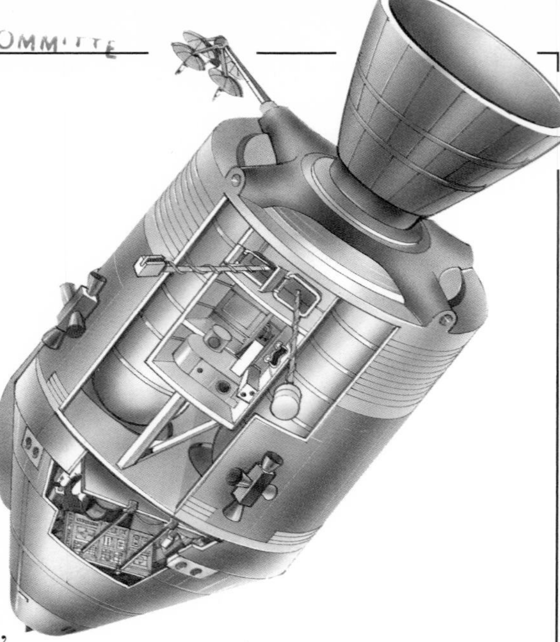

Page numbers in bold type refer to illustrations.

PRINTED IN BELGIUM BY proost INTERNATIONAL BOOK PRODUCTION